WE CAN BE FRIENDS!

A SONG ABOUT FRIENDSHIP

By VITA JIMÉNEZ

Illustrations by JANET CHEESEMAN

Music by ERIK KOSKINEN

CANTATA
LEARNING

WWW.CANTATALEARNING.COM

CANTATA
LEARNING

Published by Cantata Learning
1710 Roe Crest Drive
North Mankato, MN 56003
www.cantatalearning.com

A note to educators and librarians from the publisher: Cantata Learning has provided the following data to assist in book processing and suggested use of Cantata Learning product.

Publisher's Cataloging-in-Publication Data
Prepared by Librarian Consultant: Ann-Marie Begnaud
Library of Congress Control Number: 2016938066
    We Can Be Friends! : A Song about Friendship
    Series: Me, My Friends, My Community
    By Vita Jiménez
    Illustrations by Janet Cheeseman
    Music by Erik Koskinen
    Summary: Positive, upbeat lyrics and colorful illustrations teach children to celebrate diversity and embrace those who are different.
    ISBN: 978-1-63290-779-0 (library binding/CD)
Suggested Dewey and Subject Headings:
    Dewey: E 177.62
    LCSH Subject Headings: Friendship – Juvenile literature. | Multiculturalism – Juvenile literature. | Friendship – Songs and music – Texts. | Multiculturalism – Songs and music – Texts. | Friendship – Juvenile sound recordings. | Multiculturalism – Juvenile sound recordings.
    Sears Subject Headings: Friendship. | Multiculturalism. | School songbooks. | Children's music. |
    BISAC Subject Headings: JUVENILE NONFICTION / Social Topics / Friendship | JUVENILE NONFICTION / Music / Songbooks. | JUVENILE NONFICTION / People & Places / General

Book design and art direction: Tim Palin Creative
Editorial direction: Flat Sole Studio
Music direction: Elizabeth Draper
Music written and produced by Erik Koskinen and recorded at Real Phonic Studios

Printed in the United States of America in North Mankato, Minnesota.
072017   0367CGF17

ACCESS THE MUSIC!

SCAN CODE WITH MOBILE APP

CANTATALEARNING.COM

TIPS TO SUPPORT LITERACY AT HOME

WHY READING AND SINGING WITH YOUR CHILD IS SO IMPORTANT

Daily reading with your child leads to increased academic achievement. Music and songs, specifically rhyming songs, are a fun and easy way to build early literacy and language development. Music skills correlate significantly with both phonological awareness and reading development. Singing helps build vocabulary and speech development. And reading and appreciating music together is a wonderful way to strengthen your relationship.

READ AND SING EVERY DAY!

TIPS FOR USING CANTATA LEARNING BOOKS AND SONGS DURING YOUR DAILY STORY TIME

1. As you sing and read, point out the different words on the page that rhyme. Suggest other words that rhyme.

2. Memorize simple rhymes such as Itsy Bitsy Spider and sing them together. This encourages comprehension skills and early literacy skills.

3. Use the questions in the back of each book to guide your singing and storytelling.

4. Read the included sheet music with your child while you listen to the song. How do the music notes correlate to the words of the song?

5. Sing along on the go and at home. Access music by scanning the QR code on each Cantata book. You can also stream or download the music for free to your computer, smartphone, or mobile device.

Devoting time to daily reading shows that you are available for your child. Together, you are building language, literacy, and listening skills.

Have fun reading and singing!

Everyone is different, but we're also the same. We all want to feel like we **belong**. People can be different and still get along. We can become friends with people who are different from us if we **accept** them for who they are. Good friends will accept you for who you are, too!

Now turn the page and sing along!

I may not look the way you do,
but I can still be friends with you.

I like to feel like I belong.
I'm sure that we can get along.

I may not dress the way you do,
but I can still be friends with you.

I like to feel like I belong.
I'm sure that we can get along.

I may not **speak** the way you do,
but I can still be friends with you.

I like to feel like I belong.
I'm sure that we can get along.

I may not eat the way you do,
but I can still be friends with you.

I like to feel like I belong.

I'm sure that we can get along.

I may not act the way you do,
but I can still be friends with you.

I like to feel like I belong.
I'm sure that we can get along.

bird   el pájaro

I may not write the way you do,
but I can still be friends with you.

I like to feel like I belong.
I'm sure that we can get along.

I may not play the way you do,
but I can still be friends with you.

I like to feel like I belong.

I'm sure that we can get along.

I may not look the way you do,
but I can still be friends with you.

I like to feel like I belong.
I'm sure that we can get along.

SONG LYRICS
We Can Be Friends!

I may not look the way you do,
but I can still be friends with you.
I like to feel like I belong.
I'm sure that we can get along.

I may not dress the way you do,
but I can still be friends with you.
I like to feel like I belong.
I'm sure that we can get along.

I may not speak the way you do,
but I can still be friends with you.
I like to feel like I belong.
I'm sure that we can get along.

I may not eat the way you do,
but I can still be friends with you.
I like to feel like I belong.
I'm sure that we can get along.

I may not act the way you do,
but I can still be friends with you.
I like to feel like I belong.
I'm sure that we can get along.

I may not write the way you do,
but I can still be friends with you.
I like to feel like I belong.
I'm sure that we can get along.

I may not play the way you do,
but I can still be friends with you.
I like to feel like I belong.
I'm sure that we can get along.

I may not look the way you do,
but I can still be friends with you.
I like to feel like I belong.
I'm sure that we can get along.

We Can Be Friends!

Indie Pop
Erik Koskinen

Verse

1. I may not look the way you do, but I can still be friends with you. I like to feel like I be-long. I'm sure that we can get a-long.

Verse 2
I may not dress the way you do,
but I can still be friends with you.
I like to feel like I belong.
I'm sure that we can get along.

Verse 3
I may not speak the way you do,
but I can still be friends with you.
I like to feel like I belong.
I'm sure that we can get along.

Verse 4
I may not eat the way you do,
but I can still be friends with you.
I like to feel like I belong.
I'm sure that we can get along.

Verse 5
I may not act the way you do,
but I can still be friends with you.
I like to feel like I belong.
I'm sure that we can get along.

Verse 6
I may not write the way you do,
but I can still be friends with you.
I like to feel like I belong.
I'm sure that we can get along.

Verse 7
I may not play the way you do,
but I can still be friends with you.
I like to feel like I belong.
I'm sure that we can get along.

Verse 8
I may not look the way you do,
but I can still be friends with you.
I like to feel like I belong.
I'm sure that we can get along.

Outro

GLOSSARY

accept—to be okay with something

belong—to be part of something

speak—to say words

GUIDED READING ACTIVITIES

1. How are you different from your friends? How are they similar to you? Why is it important to like people who are different than you are?

2. Have you ever felt like you don't belong? How did it make you feel? Can you think of ways to help others feel like they belong?

3. What is your favorite food? Ask your friends what their favorite food is. Do some of them like the same things?

TO LEARN MORE

Harris, Robbie H. *Who We Are! All about Being the Same and Being Different*. Sommerville, MA: Candlewick Press, 2016.

Higgins, Melissa. *I Am Respectful*. North Mankato, MN: Capstone, 2014.

Higgins, Melissa. *We All Come from Different Cultures*. North Mankato, MN: Capstone, 2012.

Higgins, Melissa. *We All Look Different*. North Mankato, MN: Capstone, 2012.